The Seven Rules for Building Effective Analytical Models for Decisions

The Seven Rules for Building Effective Analytical Models for Decisions

Frank A. Tillman

Deandra T. Cassone

Deandra T. Cassone
Spring Hill, KS

First Printing October 2016

Book Cover Artist: http://www.selfpubbookcovers.com/RLSather

ISBN-13: 978-0692788264
ISBN-10: 0692788263

Library of Congress Control Number: 2016916795
Deandra T Cassone, Spring Hill, KS 66083

CONTENTS

Introduction

The objective is to develop robust, analytical solutions to problems and decisions facing corporations in today's competitive environment. The number of tools and methods is vast, and it is very important to recognize and understand each method that should be used in a given situation. Through years of consulting, operating our own companies, and working in a number of corporate environments, we have developed insights into which methods work and which do not in the "real world." Our numerous consulting projects and broad experience in industry have led us to the development of these fundamental rules for building analysis models to solve complex corporate problems.

At times, developing analytically based solutions can lead to results that may not be as useful as they could be for the ultimate user. Our goal with this book is to describe some common-sense principles that can be used to ensure that the models and solutions that are developed meet the decision maker's needs. We have learned these principles through our experience in various applications. We'd like to communicate these principles to you to help you avoid these mistakes and help you develop better usable solutions. These principles apply to solutions you are developing and to help you manage individuals that work for you. Either way, keeping these principles in mind will help provide analytical solutions that meet the needs of the decision makers.

Rule 1: Select the Methods That the Decision Maker Can Understand

Problem solutions must be understood by those who are going to make the decisions. Many corporations have trusted employees who understand analytical methods and how to apply them. However, if they cannot easily explain how the results were achieved to those who must act on the solutions, they will not get the support they need to implement the solutions. We have seen this a number of times in our work and would caution against overcomplicating the solutions, no matter how robust they may be.

One study, which included the allocation of limited resources, was a typical linear programming problem. We developed and used a linear programming model and obtained a number of solutions from a number of "what if" scenarios. We then took each of the solutions to the company's accounting department and had their employees verify the results. We had listed the possible scenarios and had the decision makers pick the one they liked best. We could then tell them that their accounting department employees had verified each one without having to explain how they were determined.

Management did not understand linear programming and how we arrived at the best solutions for each scenario, but they accepted the results because their accounting department verified each solution. Thus it was easy for the decision makers to accept the results. This approach can be used for any complicated analytical method and provides a way for any decision maker to accept the solution.

Communication. Solutions and the process used by the analyst to get to the solution need to be understood by the decision maker. Communication is what separates great analysts from the average analysts. Great analysts can communicate their methodology, insights, and recommendations, simply and effectively, to non-analysts and decision makers. Some decision makers may ask about the details around a model, however, if the analyst can't answer those questions simply and confidently, then the decision maker might not have confidence in the analyst or the work presented to them. As an analyst you want decision makers to have confidence and use your work to help make decisions.

Decision makers have limited time to absorb the results of an analysis. There are many issues that management faces, and they need to be able to trust you to develop solutions that they can use to solve problems and communicate up the management chain. The manager or decision maker may have to carry this analysis forward and needs to be able to explain the methodology, reasoning and results themselves. Sometimes, it is less about what you can prove, and more about what you can sell.

Over-complication. Presenting overly complicated solutions can cause decision makers to miss the message of the results. Models with complicated algorithms taking into account all variables, constraints and parameters that are presented poorly, can result in presentations that focus on the complication of the methodology, not the solution that is generated. There are times when complicated algorithms are required to solve problems, but ensuring that the methodology and data can be broken down into component parts and explained in aggregate is absolutely necessary to have the solution adopted.

Engineers and technical analysts often take problems as more complicated than the general public can understand. Problems and solutions need to be understood not only by fellow engineers, but also by the high level executives who make the decisions. If a decision maker is unable to understand your analysis, then it is very unlikely that they will support your analysis and solutions and will probably not take your recommendation very seriously.

There are multiple analytical methods that can be used to solve problems. Some of the methods need mathematical background that decision makers may not have. Some of the methods may result in multiple different solutions that may result in a compromised solution that satisfy several decision makers. When we make decisions, we have to consider the decision maker in order to select the best method or approach for decision making. Some of decisions are not so complex that they need complex methods and may be solved by very basic and simple approaches. To obtain the best decision in the process, we must account for the decision maker in the complexity of the methods used to solve the problem.

Providing results to executives when they do not fully understand how these results were achieved can result in the misinterpretation of the solution and the results that are generated. The decision maker must be confident that the solution is accurate, achievable, and believable. If you present a method that is too complicated for the decision makers they may reject the whole analysis. The analysis can be robust and highly beneficial to a company, but if you have not accounted for your audience, your analysis may never be implemented

Relationship Building. Solutions must develop confidence and understanding with the decision maker or client. Understanding what level of complexity would be acceptable to use for a company is crucial. In some cases, even the use of an Excel macro can leave a management team confused and not interested in your results.

Overly complicated solutions have the potential to even agitate your superiors, especially if they cannot understand the methods that you used. They may view you as a show-off and it might result in repercussions for your career. You must understand your audience as you develop and present solutions.

A good idea is just an idea unless it can be implemented in such a fashion that is practical and beneficial to all involved. There is a distinction made between information and intelligence. Information is simply raw data that the analyst might understand, but it needs to be formatted which allows the decision maker to understand it. A method might provide the analyst with what they are looking for, but unless they can put that information to use, then the method is not accomplishing the task.

To achieve the best possible solution, the team must have the full cooperation of every member on the team. If the entire team doesn't understand what method is being used, then they can't participate. Then a different, more simplistic approach should be used. To find the best solution, the method used must be one that every team member can understand in order to achieve full participation. These methods cannot be complicated to the decision maker and must explain how the "results were achieved." For example, a decision maker may understand a linear programming approach to a problem. Attributes such as labor costs, equipment, and materials available can be represented as linear constraints and variables, but it may be difficult understanding results in linear programming standard form. This can be related to the practice of "less is more", in which a concise presentation of how methods supports overall objectives is more effective than to clutter solutions with analytical details.

Key Points

1. **Communication.** Ensure you can communicate your model and results to your decision makers.

2. **Over-complication.** Select methods that accomplish the goals of the analysis with the least complicated methods.

3. **Relationship Building.** Selecting the right solutions can build relationship with you, clients and other members of the company.

Rule 2: The Decision Process Must Be Easy To Use and Understand

Decision processes that are complicated, have massive amounts of steps or data to process, or that are not "user friendly" will keep decision makers from using the results. It is better to select a simpler approach that is easy to apply with available data and that can be understood and provide solutions quickly.

Simpler Approaches Are Easier to Use. It is better to select a simpler approach that is easy to apply with available data and that can provide solutions quickly and are easy to use. One of General Patton's famous quotes. "A good plan violently executed right now is far better than a perfect plan executed next week." Analysts can overly complicate problems. This can delay action and require incredible amounts of effort to come up with the perfect solution. Simplicity in the decision process can help in a time constrained environment. Simplicity can also get "by-in" from non-analysts. Ultimately, we want our work to help decision makers make "good" decisions and a simple decision process is one way we can get our management to "buy in."

Simpler approaches that require less detail to generate a solution means that there is less that the decision maker needs to understand behind the model. Although this is somewhat self-explanatory, in the age of sophistication, remembering this when developing solutions for your company can make the communication of your results easier and easier to understand.

Additionally, there is an elegance in simplicity and many times, meeting the rules such as we are describing in this book can lead to the development of innovative solutions. Crafting robust and comprehensive solutions in simpler terms requires the analyst to think not only of how to generate the answer but also to develop a solution approach that addresses not only the analytics but the environment in which it will be implemented and used. The analyst cannot just throw a method at the problem, he must incorporate the environmental factors that the results will be a part of in the company and understand the goals and objectives.

Develop Tools that the Decision Maker Can Easily Understand and Use. The use of technical knowledge is a great ability. With that, not all individuals like or are willing to explore the details of a technical solution. Knowing that, the user interface between the model and the decision maker should be simple and intuitive. As an example, in much of the consulting work that we have done, we have used Multiple Attribute Decision Making models. These models have been implemented for the Joint Chief of Staff of the Army, the Air Force Materials Lab, DuPont, Frito-Lay, Hallmark Cards and others. The decision maker knew very little of this entire field of study, however, we were able to present them with simple data input screens and lead them through the process to gather the information for the decision via automated screens and menus. They then could use this user-friendly interface to explore and test their decisions without being experts in the field of Decision Science. Additionally, this also provided a means to enhance the buy-in by the decision maker on the use of the model and the results that were generated.

Develop Models that are "Fool Proof" for Users. This can be applied even in using Excel for modeling. Locking cells or macros that contain actual calculations and only allowing the user to provide the input data can help to make a solution process easy. Through the use of macros, the user should be able to click a button after submitting input data, and receive the "optimal decision". Controls should be in place to insure the input data is in an appropriate range.

Another example may be a distribution center that wants to decide which locations to ship to, how much material, how much inventory to store, etc. After building a model, the distribution center manager should be able to type in the necessary inputs like, that day's inventory, sales orders, etc. and have the excel program provide the best combination of activities for that given day. The model will not give an answer like "increase capacity and throughput" but rather, "Ship X amount of product" so there is no miscommunication in the decision making.

Key Points

1. **Simpler Approaches Are Easier to Understand.** Simpler approaches that require less detail to generate a solution means the decision maker can more easily understand how the model works.

2. **Develop Tools that the Decision Maker Can Easily Use.** Develop models with user friendly interfaces so that the decision maker can use the model and also help the buy-in to the solution.

3. **Develop Models that are "Fool Proof" for Users.** Ensure that the models you develop have the necessary functionality and protection particularly input data so that the decision maker cannot not make accidental mistakes.

Rule 3: The Model Must Fit the Time Frame Available For Development

When developing a solution to a problem, it is important to understand the time constraints and the expectations by management in regards to the solution development. Individuals in corporations are under pressure to deliver results quickly. A sophisticated model may take months to develop to solve the problem, however, management may look for a result in weeks versus months. An understanding of getting an appropriately accurate solution within the time allotted is necessary to be useful to the corporation. An example of this may be an identified need to develop a multiple objective decision making solution, however, timing is such that a simulation model that can be quickly developed and which can be used to search for better results may be all that the time allows. It is important to understand the time frame available for development to provide a solution that is of value to the organization.

Time is Critical. Time constraints are a big factor in the types of the analysis that can be done. Some models take months to gather the right data and input into the model. However, management typically wants answers much quicker. Good analysis and approximately produced solution on time is much more valuable to decision makers than a great analysis produced late or after the time the decision is needed. If a team takes a year to find a solution to a problem that needs to be fixed in a few months, then the whole process provides no value. There are multi-year problems and problems where decisions must be made in a matter of weeks. An in-depth model, although accurate, may not be completed in time to be useful, where an incomplete or directionally-correct analysis may be enough to provide the best answer.

In industry decisions must be made in a timely manner to keep projects moving forward. If the model you design cannot be solved in time to use the results to help make a decision the model is useless. This is a great opportunity for innovation because you're trying to solve the problem in a shorter amount of time which has benefits discussed in the first rule.

Outside Influences. Sometimes an organization must react to an outside influence which can severely shorten the amount of time available to develop a solution or to expand that influence. In these cases, it is critical that a method be developed to deliver the analysis and courses of action in a timely manner. This means that oftentimes the preferred method cannot be used if it requires a significant investment of time. Therefore solutions must fit into a timeline that allows the information to be of value to the decision maker. There is a time beyond which information is not of value, no matter how thorough and detailed that information or analysis is.

Completion Date. The completion date for a solution set by management should be a factor in deciding which model to use. Some analysis should be done upfront to ensure that the model can be completed in the timeframe set by management. There may be tradeoff in accuracy of the model for a faster solution that may not be as accurate but this may be required if management is not willing to provide the additional time needed for a more lengthy model. The longer the time for model development, the data has a higher probability of changing. Many times the last thing management wants to hear is a request for more time on a project when they have set a clear expectation for the need date. In order to avoid this problem, the model best available to fit the timeframe should be selected.

Frequently people have managers above them asking for results and thus this means that they are going to be looking for numbers and answers. With all of these time constraints in mind it is very important to have a variety of tools that you can implement depending upon what management is looking for. Most of the problems could be solved with more complex methods, but that development will take too much time and the company is looking for a quicker turnaround. It is important when you first meet with a client or management team to understand what their time crunches are. If a product has to be launched on a set date, or a merger is going through on a set date, then your analysis must be completed in a timely manner before that date. It is a very easy trap to fall into wanting to use your best tool to fix a problem, but if another tool can fix it adequately in a shorter amount of time, it is sometimes better to develop an adequate solution over the best solution. Time is money in business today and being a week late to a launch could cost the company large revenues and market share. Always identify your time frame and then fit your methods and data to match, not the other way around.

Key Points

1. **Time is Critical.** Industry decisions must be made in a timely fashion to stay competitive. Analysis and models must meet these constraints.
2. **Outside Influences.** Sometimes, outside influences can drive requirements for analysis and model building. Reacting to the market must be done quickly with the best possible analysis and you must factor in the availability of data.
3. **Completion Date.** Meeting completion dates are as critical as the results generated by a model. If a model or analysis cannot be completed on time, it may have no value to the corporation.

Rule 4: The Model Must Be Adaptable To an Ever-Changing Corporate Environment

Overly complex or rigid models may not be adaptable to the ever-changing corporate environment. New technologies are introduced quickly. Mergers and acquisitions may change the profile of a business. People change and move within a corporate environment so support for development may be limited to the senior executive's tenure in a position. It is important to structure models with the selected environment in mind so that these models can be adapted to solve problems quickly.

Adaptability. Due to emerging technologies and a dynamic business environment, companies must be able to adapt quickly to change. For example, companies that emerged from the .com boom in the 90's are now adapting to data analytics in support of decisions methods. In addition, social media changed the landscape on the type, access, and quantity of information people want. Advertisers use predictive analytic models to anticipate customer needs, thus decision support models need to be adaptable and relevant to their operating environment. The introduction of contemporary analytical software programs like R, VBA, SAS, Tableau, just to name a few, support the development of 'measurement and decision space' required for military decisions.

Models and analysis should be developed with the future direction of a company in mind. Understanding changes in the market place and competitors can help to anticipate future changes that may be required in an analytical effort. A big picture view of the environment can help to see how and where the analysis or model may fit into the corporate infrastructure and where it may need to be adapted in the future to meet the changing needs of the company.

Changes in Management. Changes in management and senior personnel can impact an analysis or a model. Many times these individuals will have differing views from their predecessors. Because of that, not only should a model be developed in a quick time frame, it must be adaptable to changes in management objectives. A static model can lose its utility when management changes occur. The ability to incorporate changes into your model allows it to have longevity and stay relevant with changes in management or business conditions.

Access to Model Structure. One way to allow for changes in models is to develop them such that the decision maker can easily change the underlying structure or parameters. Developing models and analysis from a variable or parameter-centric perspective will allow the decision makers to adapt it to their view and operating philosophy. For example, a production scheduling tool was created that automatically generated decisions that were previously overlooked without any analysis. The model was created with an interface that allowed non-technical users to easily change the underlying structure to adapt to changes. Had that not been the case, the tool would have been used for a couple months, and then been outdated. This approach made the tool adaptable enough to be used in the foreseeable future.

Key Points

1. **Adaptability.** Due to emerging technologies and a dynamic business environment, companies must be able to adapt quickly to change.
2. **Changes in Management**. Changes in management and senior personnel can impact a model or analysis.
3. **Access to Model Structure.** One way to allow for changes in models is to develop them such that the decision maker can easily change the underlying structure or parameters.

Rule 5: The Model Must Be Linked To Achieving the Corporate Objectives

It is important to have a clear understanding of corporate objectives when developing a model. Without that understanding, solutions generated by the effort may not support the strategic direction of the company.

Understand the Corporate Objectives Before You Begin. Before you begin to build a model it is important to understand the overarching direction of a company. For example, if you are working for a company who is looking to double the size of their market share in the next ten years and your model comes back with an optimal solution to reduce the amount of inventory and give up a small portion of the market share to cut costs, management will not support this decision at all.

It is important to understand the objectives of the company before you build the model because only then can you develop a model that works towards achieving the specific goals. Without this understanding before building a model, you may come up with a solution that does not support the strategic objectives. A solution that does not support the goals of the company is not a solution at all, and time is wasted building a model that adds no value.

May Result in a Model that Requires Rework or is Unusable. If a model is not supporting the overall corporate objective, the company may not accept your solution or you may be required to rework your analysis. It is important for management teams to know that the results or solutions that you have generated will move them in the same direction that the company is heading. Spend time getting to know management and where they are heading before making any decisions regarding what model you would like to build.

If a model is developed that is not in line with corporate objectives, time may be required to rework and redo the model. In order to save rework or project failure, time should be spent up front to make sure there is alignment before beginning the assignment. One benefit by making sure corporate objectives are considered in the model is that the model can be used to communicate the objectives to other members in the organization.

An example of this occurred when developing a model for an airline catering firm. The model was developed to maximize profit and recommendations were made to reduce inventory and facilities. Certain senior level executives did not participate in the model definition phase and their input on corporate objectives was not included in the model development. When the study was presented, we were told that the corporate objectives were not to maximize profit, but to maximize sales because the company was going public. Significant rework on the analysis was required to provide the results and solutions in line with the new corporate objectives.

Know the Importance of the Objectives. It's important that the decision makers know the corporate objective and the associated importance of each of the goals and objectives. Sometimes the time matters, sometimes costs matter, and sometimes the quality of the product is important. For example, in introducing the new product to the market, corporations have to make their important decisions in selecting which product and which design to introduce. For the group of decision makers, it is important to know the objection of the corporate clearly to define and select the method and the process of decision making correctly. With certain methods, decision makers can define attributes and for each attribute they can define weights which reflect their importance in the view of decision makers. Weights and attributes should be in the direction of the corporate objective. When time is an important item in decision making, it makes sense to give higher weight to time as one of the attributes in the process of decision making.

Key Points

1. **Understand the Corporate Objectives Before You Begin.** Before you begin to build a model it is important to understand the overarching direction of a company and where it is going.

2. **May Result in a Model that Requires Rework or is Unusable.** If a model is not built with all executives (decision makers) inputs that support the overall corporate objective, the company may not

accept your solution or you may be required to rework your analysis.

3. **Know the Importance of the Objectives.** It's important that the decision makers know the corporate objective, the associated importance of each of the goals and objectives and the metrics to measure each.

Rule 6: Lack of Data Can Be Supplemented With Expert Opinion

Sometimes a corporate environment or activities are changing so rapidly that using historical data to forecast future activities will result in an inaccurate forecast. In those cases, expert opinion can be used to supplement or replace historical data in forecasting. Group decision making methods presented in *The Science of Common Sense: Best Practical Decision Making Methods* can provide a structured approach to capturing this forward-looking forecast information from corporate experts.

When data is unavailable, limited, full of errors, or might take too long to generate, some supplementation with expert opinion can help to frame initial analysis or even provide insight as to the context that limited data provides. This is especially true in forecasting or trying to account for the actions of competitors or strategic enemies, who are themselves using available data to reach conclusions. Expert group panels are particularly helpful in providing insight and generating additional alternatives when prediction is uncertain.

Data is Unavailable. There are times when only historical data is available, and that data might not necessarily reflect the situation or be useful for indicating future trends. It is necessary to have the opinions of experts in that particular region or field who can provide the knowledge that simple data cannot. This is relevant when decisions need to be made with regards to human behavior or relationships. Although human behavior can be categorized or seems predictable in certain instances, the fact remains that humans are individuals and oftentimes only another person who understands their experiences can provide the best information.

This also supports an ever changing corporate environment. New products and processes are introduced. New competitors arise with no historical reference. There may be no way to model these circumstances with historical information.

One military example is a study for the integration of women into Ranger School. The Army collected various data points about the physical dexterity of women and also the results of women in similar training.

However, an important part of the study was input from senior leaders who had experience at Ranger School, leading mixed gender units, and leading strictly male units. Information was gained from a quantifiable basis, however, surveys and discussion points for the proposed integration of women into special operations forces occurred with senior leaders. In this case, expert opinion from practitioners is necessary and useful to supplement data.

Using Historical Data May Result in Inaccurate Forecasts. Relying mainly in historical data to forecast future activities can result in inaccurate forecast. The recruitment of consultants and subject matter experts can leverage gaps in data or overreliance in "historical experience". In 2009, George Friedman wrote a bestselling book: "The Next 100 Years. A forecast for the 21st Century", the author cites historical trends to make predictions of future events. In his introduction, the author caveats that if his claims turn out to be "fifty percent correct" in the least, then significant catastrophic events are expected to occur for the remaining part of this century. The author does not claim to be an expert but relies on "historical events" to predict changes in the world geopolitical context as the cause of future events.

Group Decision Making Techniques Can Be Used to Gather Expert Opinion. Although some analysts may be hesitant to use expert opinion, there are a number of methods and a field of study that can be used to develop estimates from experts. These methods help to gather this information in a structured way using set processes. Hesitancy in using expert opinion in analyses and models can be reduced by using a structured way to capture and utilize this information in an analytical model.

Key Points

1. **Data is Unavailable**. There are times when only historical data is available, and that data might not necessarily reflect the situation or be useful for indicating future trends.

2. **Using Historical Data May Result in Inaccurate Forecasts.**
    Relying mainly in historical data to forecast future activities can
    result in inaccurate forecast.

3. **Group Decision Making Techniques Can Be Used to Gather
    Expert Opinion.** Although some analysts may be hesitant to use
    expert opinion, there are a number of methods and a field of study
    that can be used to develop estimates from experts.

Rule 7: Definition of the Optimal Solution

Sometimes when we develop models and solutions, we look for extreme levels of accuracy and improvement within the organization. This may require months of development time and pressure to show ultimate results when the model and solutions are delivered. In our experience, we have redefined an optimal solution to be "Are we doing this better than before in regards to corporate objectives?" Incremental improvements to operations and processes provide value to an organization and their bottom line. Providing the right level of detail and accuracy within a given time frame can show value in the processes and also be a win for structured analytical processes.

Rarely will a complex problem have a simple or single best solution. The best solution or set of solutions might entail several tradeoffs or risk mitigation strategies to compensate for unknowns or costs in an attempt to maximize benefits. Sensitivity analysis can help to identify tipping points where one solution becomes dominated by another. Some attributes are not necessarily tangible, such as a decision regarding layoffs to cut operational costs, which might have a political or social repercussion.

Don't Be Obsessed with Analytical Gymnastics. As technical personnel, we are often obsessed with the correct or most optimal value of a project, like a linear programming model. The optimal solution is an improvement of the current situation. This contrasts with the mindset of linear programming where the best solution is the main goal. To agree on an optimal solution, it is important to agree on the objectives of the modeling project before beginning. Both parties involved should agree that the objective is to maximize profit, or minimize scrapped product, etc. This avoids miscommunication in model building.

Know What Constitutes Success from the Decision Maker. Understanding what the decision maker views as a great solution is key to understanding an optimal result. It is important to understand what "optimal" means to the decision maker, the stakeholders and the analysis team. "Optimal" does not always mean the best, but can mean better or the best available under certain conditions and constraints.

Incremental Improvements Provide Value to a Corporation. Based on the fast-paced environment, time-frames for model development, changes in the corporate environment and other factors, incremental improvements provide value to a corporation. A complex solution that cannot be implemented has no value compared to an incremental solution that is implemented. Do not let a method or complex analysis overtake the value of improvements to an organization.

Key Points
1. **Don't Be Obsessed with Analytical Gymnastics.** As technical personnel, we are often obsessed with the correct or most optimal value of a project, like a linear programming model. The optimal solution is an improvement of the current situation.
2. **Know What Constitutes Success from the Decision Maker.** Understanding what the decision maker views as a great solution is key to understanding an optimal result.
3. **Incremental Improvements Provide Value to a Corporation.** Based on the fast-paced environment, time-frames for model development, changes in the corporate environment and other factors, incremental improvements may provide the only achievable value to the corporation.

Conclusions

In a fast-paced analytical world with myriads of data and analytical techniques, it is important to remember some fundamentals in developing solutions that can be of real value to your corporation. As analysts, engineers and technical experts, we tend to get enthralled with the methods themselves and not the generation of solutions that provide value to the organization in the time frame that is required.

The goal of this book is to provide some lessons-learned, based on our experience to assist you in your career. If you can avoid one mistake, we feel like we have been successful with this book.

About the Authors

Frank A. Tillman, PhD, PE, has a varied career of over thirty years in academia, consulting, and real estate development. He served as department head at Kansas State University for more than twenty years, where he published over fifty professional articles and five books. He has also authored several books for professionals identifying the approaches that work best for solving problems and offering practicable solutions.

Deandra T. Cassone, PhD, PMP, serves as an associate professor in the Industrial and Manufacturing Systems Engineering program at Kansas State University and has been in management at a Fortune 100 company. Her career of over thirty years includes consulting, technical, and management roles and has published three books. With an interest in building structured decision making models, she has been awarded numerous business process patents.

Acknowledgements

We would like to acknowledge our family and friends for their review and comments on the content in this book. Additionally, we'd like to acknowledge the students in the spring semester Multiple Criteria Decision Making course at Kansas State University for their comments, thoughts and examples in regards to these rules.

Dedication

Frank A. Tillman, PhD, PE
July 22, 1937 – February 26, 2017

Frank was born July 22, 1937 in Linn, Missouri. The unfortunate early passing of his father started him working at the age of nine. This work ethic carried throughout his life. Frank was an athlete through high school and went to college at Lincoln University on a basketball scholarship. He soon realized that academia was his passion. Frank was married to Barbara Langendoerfer and they shared 58 years together at the time of his death. Working full-time to support his family and going to school full-time he earned a Bachelors and Master's Degree in Industrial Engineering from the University of Missouri. He worked at Standard Oil of Ohio and attended Case Institute working on his Ph.D. in Operations Research. He was awarded a Ford Foundation grant to finish his Ph.D. at the University of Iowa in Industrial Engineering.

After graduating, he moved his family to Manhattan, Kansas and took a position as a Professor at Kansas State University. A year later, at 29, he became Head of the Department of Industrial Engineering. Frank loved academics. He mentored many students throughout his career that have become very successful and kept in touch with him over time. As Professor and Department Head, he was instrumental in the approval of the engineering PhD program, he was a founder of the KSU Chapter of Tau Beta Pi, and was involved in Alpha Pi Mu, ABET accreditation, was an Institute of Industrial Engineering fellow, wrote fifty-four papers and two books during his time on the faculty and was awarded emeritus status upon his departure from the university. Frank was also inducted into the KSU Engineering Hall of Fame. Frank began his real estate development career during this time as well, developing a number of housing communities in Manhattan, Kansas. In 1972, he received a Presidential appointment to U.S. President Nixon's Price Commission and moved his family to Washington DC for a short time.

He began consulting businesses which drew him from academia to the business world as his primary career. He operated two successful consulting companies with many contracts with government agencies and Fortune 500 companies. He spent the next twenty years managing these firms with offices in Manhattan and Washington DC. Frank also continued his real estate activities with commercial and residential real estate. In Frank's later years, he published four books and four eBooks documenting his approach to problem solving and applying theory to practical solutions.

Frank was very active in the community. He served two terms on the USD 383 School Board, served on multiple advisory councils and coached numerous basketball, softball and baseball teams. His Youth Activities Foundation supported numerous sports teams in Manhattan and Kansas City. Frank and Barbara additionally support a scholarship fund for Industrial Engineering students and were Seaton Founders for the College of Engineering. One of his most treasured activities was coffee in the morning with KSU faculty and community members.

Of all of his abilities and passions, his family was always first and foremost to him. He was a man that cared for his family deeply and provided for them unceasingly. He was very involved in their lives and was happy to take them on family vacations to Disney World, ski trips, the Lake of the Ozarks and helping his kids and grandkids through college.

Frank touched many lives in his time here on earth, including students, athletes, business community members, faculty and friends. He always saw potential in people who were discouraged in engineering. He endlessly recruited for the Industrial Engineering Department. He always had an opinion and was happy to discuss it with you.

For me personally, he was my father, my mentor and my friend and he is deeply missed.

Deandra Cassone, PhD, PMP

Related Publications from the Authors

A Professional's Guide to Decision Science and Problem Solving: An Integrated Approach for Assessing Issues, Finding Solutions, and Reaching Corporate

The Science of Common Sense: Best Practical Decision Science Methods

Evaluating Products and Projects to Meet Corporate Objectives

Developing a Warehouse and Inventory Level Optimization System

Investment Strategy for Product Development in the Aerospace Industry

Manpower Requirements for Management and Professional Personnel

Strategic Planning and New Product Development

www.ingramcontent.com/pod-product-compliance
Lightning Source LLC
Chambersburg PA
CBHW060502210326
41520CB00015B/4065